During his lifetime, Bruce Lee did more to bring the martial arts to the attention of the general public than any other twentieth century man, and as a result much has been written about him. Unfortunately, the material has almost always centered around his career as a "martial artist" and "superstar." No one has ever really taken the time to look beyond the image and see him as he really was. We regard this as a blatant oversight and are determined to rectify it.

Grace Lee, Bruce's mother, has dug deeply into her private collection of family albums filled with previously unreleased photographs. Combining these with in-depth interviews of her, other family members, friends, and students, we have painted a verbal and visual portrait of the man no one knew. You will learn of his frustrations and triumphs, and see how their effect shaped his personality, driving him ever onward to fulfill the destiny he felt so strongly to be his.

For all those involved in this project, it has been a labor of love. What you as the reader are about to experience is the end result, our way of paying homage to a man blessed with a charismatic magic and a talent and wisdom far beyond his years.

Bruce Lee is gone, but in the hearts and minds of all those he touched, he will live on forever.

Acknowledgments

Unique Publications wishes to extend special thanks to the following people for their dedication and efforts in compiling this special edition: Grace Lee, Robert Lee, Agnes Lee, Phoebe Lee, Peter Lee, Dick Hennessey, Jim Serrett, Mark Komuro, Dave King, Norman Borine, Randy Wong, Rocco Zappia, Jr., and James Lew.

Photo Credits

We wish to extend our thanks to: Grace Lee, Robert Lee, Agnes Lee, Phoebe Lee, Peter Lee, Dan Lee, Dan Inosanto, Norman Borine, Randy Wong, George Foon, Warner Bros., Paramount T.V., and Columbia Studios.

Distributed exclusively by

copyright © 1986 by CFW Enterprises

UNIQUE PUBLICATIONS, 4201 VANOWEN PLACE, BURBANK, CA 91505

The Beginning

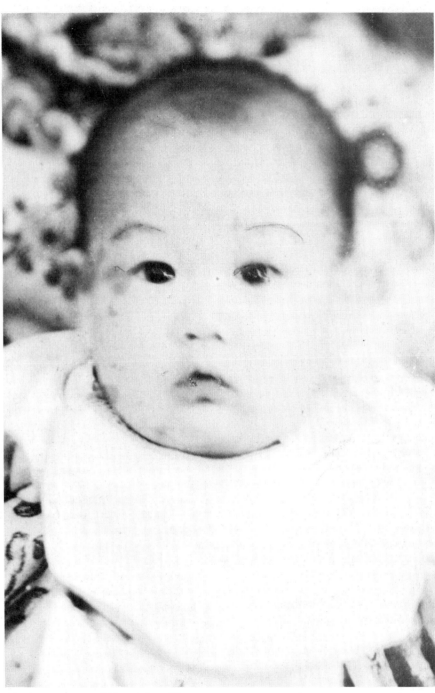

On the morning of November 27, 1940 (in the Chinese year of the Dragon), Lee Jun Fan was born in San Francisco under the supervision of Dr. Mary Glover. The mother, Grace, had not planned on an American name, and the father, at the time, was performing in New York. So it was Dr. Glover who thought of the name Bruce. The mother concurred and from then on it was Bruce Lee.

In 1939, Lee Hoi Chuen, an extremely popular entertainer in the Chinese opera brought his wife Grace, son Peter, and daughters Phoebe and Agnes from their home in Hong Kong to San Francisco. He was to appear there in a Chinese play. While still there on November 27, 1940 another son, Bruce, was born. When Bruce was only three months old, he was a baby stand-in in "Golden Gate Girl," an American production. Shortly afterward, the family returned to Hong Kong.

Bruce was a very sweet, good-natured child and when he was about four years old, Phoebe, Agnes and he all had little walk-on parts in a Chinese war play. It was probably then that Bruce consciously fell in love with acting. Being so young, he naturally didn't get too many opportunities to perform after that, but the seed had been firmly planted. From that time on, every chance he got he would visit his father on movie sets, and each time everyone would fall in love with him. Little did anyone know that before too long a career leading to superstardom would begin to blossom.

When Bruce was six years old, the director of his father's latest film saw him on the set and was so impressed that he offered him a part. His creative instincts instantly told him that there was something very "special" about Bruce. At first both Bruce and his father thought he was joking, but he assured them he was serious. Bruce, wide eyed, open mouthed, and deliriously happy, immediately accepted, and a career that would eventually lead to roles in over twenty films was launched.

Even then audiences sensed Bruce's intense energy and love of life. As he steadily grew in popularity, so did his driving compulsion to continually search for new ways to channel his energy. One such way was that Bruce, who had always told tall tales and funny stories, gradually became

Bruce was born in San Francisco while his father, Lee Hoi Chuen, an extremely popular Chinese opera star, was performing in a New York play. One night fter his show Lee, well known for his comedic talent and goodnatured sense of humor playfully "initiated" Bruce into the world of entertainment. Later, when Bruce's mother saw her infant son's innocent and smiling face wildly decorated with brightly colored stage make up she was at first furious. But as she watched Bruce giggling happily as he stared in the mirror at himself (obviously loving what he saw), even she had to smile.

something of a practical joker, engineering simultaneously playful and diabolically clever pranks.

However, according to Bruce's mother, as mischievous as Bruce was, that's how good-natured he was. "One day, I walked into our living room and saw him intently looking out the window down into the street. Suddenly he started running toward the door. I asked him where he was going in such a hurry but he didn't answer and just raced out. I walked over to the window to see what he had been looking at and saw him helping a blind man across the busy street. He later told me that everyone else was just walking past the poor man and he looked so sad and frustrated that he felt he had to do something."

One instance that Grace vividly remembered occurred when Bruce's sister, Phoebe, was with him. Grace was in the kitchen when Phoebe raced in and told her Bruce was dying. Grace couldn't believe her ears, so with Phoebe tugging at her, Grace followed her into the living room and found Bruce jumping around like a crazy man clutching his throat. He was screaming, "Mommy I'm dying! I'm going to die."

Pintsize warriors Bruce and older brother Peter do battle in Hong Kong in 1945(top right). Peter and he were always very close. Robert, Agnes, Bruce, Peter, and Phoebe in Hong Kong in 1950 (Right), Agnes told us "I always sensed something special about Bruce even as a small child. He was always so positive. I knew he was going to make something of his life." Bruce's father, Lee Hoi Chuen(Below) in one of his many stage roles.

It turns out that Bruce had swallowed the rubber nipple from brother Robert's baby bottle. Grace tried to calm him, saying there was really nothing to worry about. After all, he wasn't gagging. Of course, the nipple would have to come out, so a family doctor was summoned. When he arrived, Grace explained the problem, and using sound medical advise, the doctor prescribed what he felt to be a most effective remedy . . . Ex Lax!

Agnes (who Bruce called "Little Queen") added that "As a youngster, aside from having nightmares, Bruce was a sleepwalker. We slept in bunkbeds, and many times I would see him climb down from the top bunk in the middle of the night, and while in a sound sleep, go strolling off."

As time passed, Bruce's energy began to be channelled negatively by his

An early shot of Bruce sporting a then very fashionable greasy "flat top" hairstyle. (Below)Bruce standing with his mother Grace and some friends in Hong Kong.

growing involvement with street gangs. Agnes recalled that "When Bruce was very young, I called him Little Dragon. He was always very protective, and if a boy was teasing me he would immediately come to my defense. At times like this, I was flattered and very proud of him. But as a teenager he began to get into more and more fights, for no reason at all. And if he didn't win, he was furious! He always considered himself a winner, and losing even occasionally was unbearable to him."

It was about this time that Bruce began studying Wing Chun, an extremely sophisticated Chinese self defense system. He instantly fell in love with the art and threw himself into it wholeheartedly. He practiced long and hard and became increasingly proficient. Bruce's sister Phoebe, who called him "Sai Fun" (Small Phoenix) said, "He was always trying to teach me how to break bricks but I never could."

When Bruce turned fourteen, he discovered still another way to divert his excessive energy.

He discovered the art of "dancing." With his natural grace and agility, he quickly learned all the popular dances, his favorite being the Cha Cha. Every

Bruce(top) holding up the first fish he ever caught. In another photo taken right afterward(below), you immediately sense and clearly see Bruce's intensely positive and confident attitude. It was always so noticeable that he greatly impressed everyone he met.

day after school he would go over to the home of his friend, Pearl Cho, and they would practice. In time he became the Hong Kong Cha Cha champion, winning trophy after trophy.

But still the street fighting continued, and whenever Bruce got into trouble, his mother would have to go down to school and talk to his principal. She said, "Bruce loved and respected his father and knew how much his father hated violence. I would always threaten to tell on him if he didn't start behaving. He always promised to, but he kept fighting."

About that same time, Bruce was attending St. Francis Xavier School and one of the brothers, Brother Edward, also noticed Bruce was getting very wild. To teach him a lesson in humility, he invited Bruce to go to the boxing room and put on the gloves with him in a friendly match. Bruce had never boxed before, but using Wing Chun techniques, he was able to hold his own. Seeing that Bruce had talent, he invited him to join the boxing team. He did and at a tournament shortly afterward, he defeated the boy who had been champion three years in a row.

All along, Bruce had continued to make movies in Hong Kong and his last

Bruce taking a break with an actress friend between scenes from one of his Hong Kong movies.

Bruce(top row, 8th from left) at his graduation from LaSalle Junior High School in Hong Kong(below).

one "Orphan" was received extremely favorably. As a result, Run Run Shaw, an extremely powerful producer, wanted to sign Bruce to do movies for him. It was then that Bruce, who never really liked school, announced to his mother that he wanted to quit high school and accept Shaw's offer. He felt certain that he could become a star. Grace also believed he could be successful, but was deeply concerned about what was happening to him. For one thing, he was becoming more and more involved in street fighting. Also, she felt it was very important for him to finish high school and get his diploma, The situation finally came to a head when Bruce was picked up by the police for fighting. For Grace, this was the final straw. She forbade him to accept Shaw's offer, and in 1959 sent him to live with friends in the United States, where he would finish high school. She knew in her heart that leaving would be his only chance to straighten out and make something of his life.

(Opposite page) A dapper Bruce in a later school photo.

There was a time when Bruce thought he was going to become a great singer. In fact, with his father's connections, he and the rest of his brothers and sisters were given auditions. After the auditions were over, Bruce was told not to go into singing as a career. If he did he would probably starve to death. Singing's loss was the martial arts gain.

Bruce(top)at 13 in Hong Kong. (Below) Bruce;(2nd row, 3rd from left) in a class picture at St. Francis Xavier High School.

The Practical Joker

When Bruce first began his career as a practical joker, he wasn't particularly imaginative. Sometimes he would merely sprinkle itching powder on some unsuspecting victim and almost burst trying to keep from smiling as it took effect. However, as Bruce grew older, his pranks became infinitely more sophisticated. Grace, Bruce's mother, recalls one instance in particular: "One night, when our maid went out for the evening, he moved all the furniture in her room to different spots. When she returned and stepped inside, she immediately began to stumble over things. The nearest light was in the center of the room so she banged and bumped into almost every chair and table till she reached it, switched it on, and saw where everything was. Afterward, she was furious and came to me saying she knew it was Bruce. I promised I would talk to him about it but found it very hard to keep from laughing myself."

Robert also mentioned Bruce's penchant for practical jokes. As a child he had been the victim of many of them and vividly recalled one instance in particular. "One day Bruce came into my room and told me he had invented a new game. It was called "Submarine." I, of course, asked him if he would teach me how to play it. At the time I didn't know that this was going to be a big mistake. He left the room for a few moments and came back with a sports jacket. He threw it over my head and told me to hold up the arm sleeve and look through it. Then he said that I was the submarine and the sleeve was the periscope. Other enemy vessels were all around me (his hands would serve as the enemy vessels), and if I saw one I should yell 'fire one.' The game began and when I saw his hand pass the arm hole, I yelled 'fire one.' He said I was too slow and had missed. Again his hand passed by and I yelled again, this time faster and louder. Still he said I had missed, but he was willing to give me one more chance. This time I was determined to win. I intently watched the arm hole, waiting for what seemed like hours, though it was only about twenty seconds. Finally, the hand flew past, and I screamed 'fire one.' Not only did he tell me I had missed again, but one of the enemy vessels had dropped a

depth charge on me. At that moment, Bruce poured a whole pitcher of ice water down the arm sleeve drenching me."

Agnes said, "Bruce was very mischievous as a child. One thing he liked to do was to send the maids to the store for ridiculous things he knew the stores didn't carry."

Phoebe said, "Once he handed me a book and told me I should read it because it was very special. There was no title on the book cover and I was curious to see what it was about. Upon opening the book I received an ELECTRIC SHOCK. Bruce laughed and hurriedly ran away.

Also, Bruce was always talking as a child. He was never quiet. With his tall tales and wonderful sense of humor, he was always able to make me laugh even when I was unhappy."

(Opposite page)Always funloving Bruce loved to make people laugh by dressing in outlandish costumes.

(Top)Decked out in war paint and armed with his trusty scalping knife, nine year old Bruce is all set for "cowboys and Indians" with a friend. (Below)Bruce and his sister Phoebe share some cake as Bruce's dog eyes them both intently. Bruce's practical jokes sometimes backfired. Sister Phoebe recalls the time he use to keep pushing her in the pool. Finally it wasn't funny any more to her, so she turned the tables on Bruce. She held his head underwater util he promised not to do it any more. After that Bruce decided his swimming days were over. He rarely went into a pool after that.

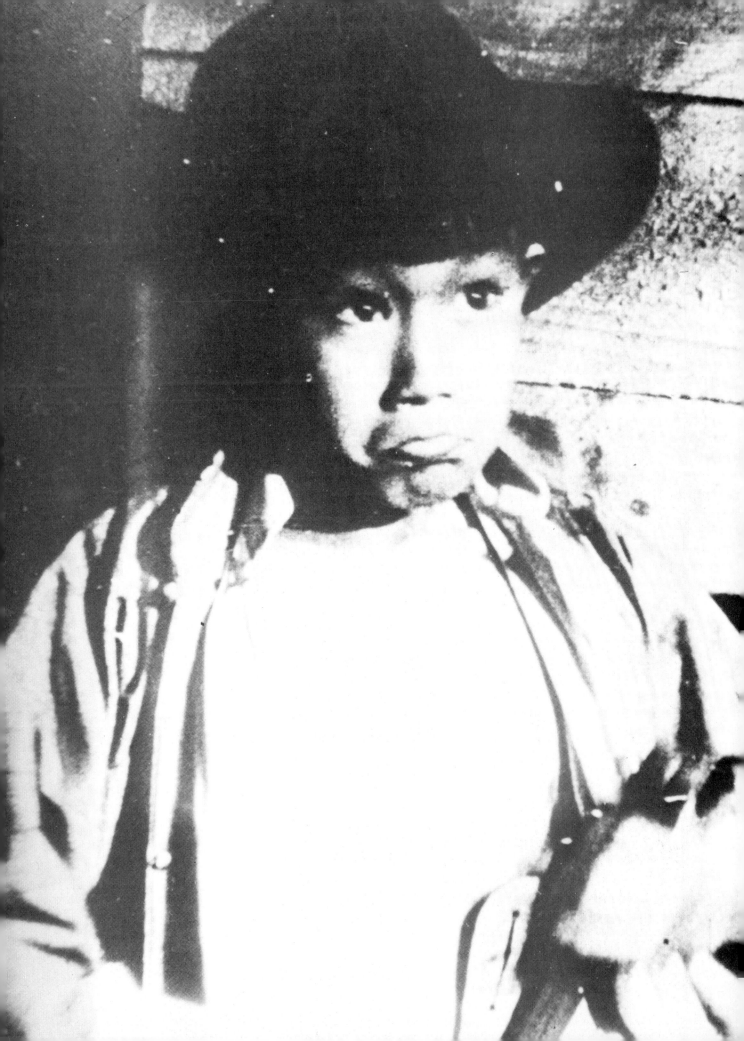

The Child Star

Bruce's Hong Kong film career began when he was only six years old. While visiting his father, Lee Hoi Chuen, on the set of his latest film, the director spotted Bruce and immediately sensed something "special" about him. He was certain beyond a doubt that audiences would fall in love with Bruce and even went so far as to offer him a role in his father's film. This was the beginning, leading to over twenty motion picture roles and steadily increasing popularity among Hong Kong audiences.

Robert also related the following story: "Whenever Bruce made a movie, he would always take some of the money he received and buy himself something. One time he bought himself a little monkey. It was not a very friendly monkey and I personally didn't even like it. It was about this time that our cousin Frank was keeping his pet bird with us for awhile. One day, the monkey somehow got out of its cage and into the bird's, ripping it to pieces. Later, our cousin came to pick it up and found it dead. He knew the monkey was the culprit, and in a fit of rage literally beat the monkey up. This made the monkey so mad that he bit me. When Bruce came home, my mother told him what had happened, and that the monkey had to go. Bruce considered the monkey merely a victim of circumstances and didn't want to give it up at first, but finally agreed to begrudgingly."

A pouty six year old Bruce Lee(opposite) made his Hong Kong film debut in 1946.

Audiences loved his emotion-charged facial expressions and scrappy personality.

13

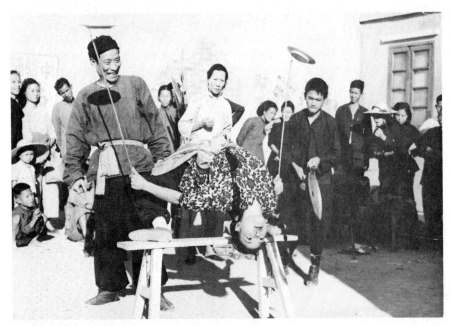

Whether Bruce played an angelic child or a devilish one didn't seem to matter to his fans. He could be underdog or aggressor, and it eventually reached the point where storylines didn't matter anymore. The fans rooted for Bruce no matter what.

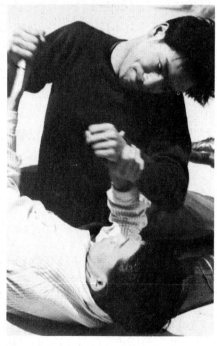

15

As Bruce grew older his popularity steadily increased. He developed a look and presence all his own and was rapidly becoming the Bruce Lee that would years later charm millions. Hong Kong audiences already were beginning to sense his intense charisma and couldn't get enough of him.

*His last Hong Kong movie "Orphan"
(above) was an enormous success.*

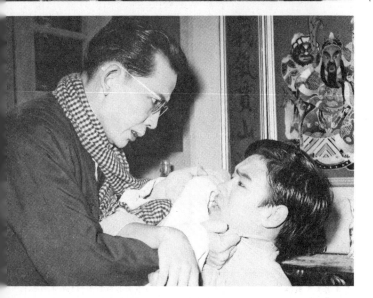

Martial Arts Beginnings

(Top)This photo of Bruce playfully sparring with his father, Lee Hoi Chuen, is
not only rare but extremely ironic as
well. It seems that Bruce's father(himself a popular entertainer and versed in
the art of Tai Chi Chuan) not only did
not want his son to be an actor but didn't
even want him to become involved in Kung
Fu. He knew well the uncertainty of show
business. He also felt that the devastating
effects of Kung Fu when applied in real
combat could make his son many enemies.
He just wanted Bruce to have a normal job
and a normal life, not hurting anyone or
himself.

Bruce began studying Wing Chun, a highly
sophisticated Chinese self defense system
under Yip Man.

Wing Chun (meaning "beautiful springtime") is a very sophisticated Chinese fighting system stressing economy of movement and springing energy. It was reportedly founded by a woman, Yim Wing Chun, over four hundred years ago. The style was based on the techniques of Shaolin nun Ng Mui of the Fukien province. Yim Wing Chun felt that Ng Mui's style was too complex and placed too much emphasis on power techniques and strong stances. She was searching for the simplest, most efficient method of defense, and not finding it among existing systems, she came up with her own.

The style that she developed was passed down through the centuries to Leong Bok Sul, Wong Wah Bo, Leong Yee Tai, Leong Jon, Chan Wah Soon, Yip Man (Bruce's instructor), Leong Sheong, and Wong Soon Sum.

Bruce had studied several different styles of kung-fu prior to Wing Chun but eventually chose it over all the others because he felt it to be the most effective. He immediately showed natural talent, and under the expert tutelage of Yip Man, he steadily improved.

Bruce started training in the martial arts mainly to overcome his fear of being humiliated in a street fight. A recollection by his sister Agnes reflects this thought; "As a teenager he began to get into more and more fights for no reason at all. And if he didn't win he was furious! He always considered himself a winner, and losing even once in a while was unbearable to him." As a result, under master Yip Man's Wing Chun teachings, Bruce became a proficient martial artist, not to mention a feared street fighter.

When Bruce joined the St. Francis Xavier boxing team, a tournament was coming up and Brother Edward felt that the team could use him. Bruce agreed to join, but refused to train. Even then, he was determined to do everything his way. And his way worked!

At the tournament, he was pitted against the boy who had been boxing champion three years in a row. Suddenly, in the middle of the fight he found himself forced up against the ropes and an instant later knocked down by one of his opponent's punches. Enraged and loudly swearing, he staggered to his feet. Then with an almost maniacal determination, he went after his adversary. Needless to say at the end of the bout a new champion had been crowned.

Though momentarily on the ropes in this 1957 tournament bout, Bruce went on to win this one and many others.

21

The Dancer

When Bruce was about fourteen, he discovered that "dancing" could be a great deal of fun. With his natural grace and knack for quickly and effortlessly picking things up, in no time at all he had learned all the popular dances. His favorite was the cha cha, and he spent many hours practicing extremely complex dance routines. He eventually became the Hong Kong Cha Cha Champion.

At 14, Bruce became interested in dancing. He had a real knack for it and rapidly became quite polished, never lacking eager partners. Much of the balance and footwork became evident in his later fighting style.

(Opposite page)In 1959, on a ship bound for the United States, Bruce dances with with a female passenger.

No one really knows if Bruce Lee was really interested in dancing or took it up because of his fondness for a girl Pearl Cho. Whatever reason Bruce had for taking up dancing he could usually be found at Pearl Cho's practicing. Later he won several cha cha contests in Hong Kong as well as in the United States.

Bruce gives his younger brother a few pointers.

Journey to the West

While in the United States, Bruce finished high school and went on to college. He never asked his mother or father for any financial assistance. By day he attended the University of Washington and nights he worked as a busboy in a restaurant. After a few months of this, he decided that this lifestyle was not for him. He quit his job at the restaurant and began teaching kung-fu. Linda Emery, a pretty blonde coed, enrolled in his class and in 1964 they were married. Shortly afterward, they moved to California.

At the age of twenty-two, Bruce authored an extremely unique text which he titled "CHINESE GUNG-FU: The Philosophical Art of SELF-DEFENSE." This book reflected his preoccupation with spiritual as well as physical development.

In 1965, Bruce's son, Brandon, was born. A short time later Bruce's father died and Bruce returned to Hong Kong for the funeral. At the funeral, Bruce was the first of the Lee children to arrive. And as was custom, he entered on his knees. He was crying uncontrollably. It was a way of asking his father for forgiveness on behalf of the rest of the family, and, at the same time, it was a way of paying respect to someone he had so deeply respected.

In 1966, Bruce landed the role of Kato in the "Green Hornet" television series and acquired an incredible following. He felt certain this was going to be his "Big Break," but after the "Green Hornet" series went off the air after only one season, Bruce found that parts calling for orientals were few and far between. He landed a small role in "Marlowe," a feature film starring James Garner, and also appeared in a few episodes of "Longstreet," a television series starring James Franciscus, but for the most part his career was going nowhere.

He was approached by promoters to open up a highly commercial, nationwide chain of "Kato's Gung-Fu

(Opposite page)Bruce standing outside Ruby Chow's, a popular Seattle restaurant. While he was staying in Seattle Bruce was allowed to live in the restaurant's attic in exchange for his services as a busboy and waiter.

Bruce standing with his mother, father, and some friends of the family.

schools" but refused (even though he really could have used the money) because he didn't feel it was the correct way to promote his art. Instead, he opened up three kwoons (schools) designed for only the most serious of martial arts students. It was here that he developed and taught what was to become JEET KUNE DO.

In 1969, word came that reruns of "The Green Hornet" had martial arts fans by the millions in Hong Kong clamoring for more, especially when they found that Kato was a homegrown product.

Knowing that Hong Kong production methods were at best "primitive," Bruce began devouring every book and bit of information dealing with film making that he could get his hands on. He felt that a once-in-a-lifetime opportunity was being laid before him and he was not about to let it slip through his fingers. He studied

(Top right)Bruce in 1960. (Bottom left) Bruce with sister Agnes in San Francisco. Agnes told us, "when Bruce was a-bout 18 he went to a fortune teller in Hong Kong. The fortune teller told him that someday he would be very rich and famous. We laughed about it but I always felt it was going to happen."

Bruce, older brother Peter, and Bobo in Seattle.

Bruce in San Francisco.

Throughout most of Bruce's teen years, he wore glasses. From the time he was seven or eight years old he had been nearsighted. "He used to spend hours in bed reading comic books with small type without my permission," recalls Grace Lee. "I think that is what contributed to his poor eyesight."

One day when he was about 12 he was riding on a bus and not wear-ing the glasses. He was eating dates, and when he was through, he threw them out of what he thought was an open window, needless to say the window was closed and the dates bounced off the glass strik-ing a rather nicely dressed male pas-senger. The man angrily turned to Bruce shouting, "what's the matter with you, are you blind or something?" An em-barrassed Bruce replied, "without my glasses, I guess I am."

direction, lighting, camera techniques, editing, and production.

The beginning of the seventies saw Bruce spending more and more time between Hollywood and Hong Kong.

Offers began pouring in from many different sources and he was continually in transit firming up commitments and scouting locations for future projects. In constant demand, his fees escalated accordingly to such astronomical rates as $275.00 per hour. However, the perpetuation of Jeet Kune Do was still very important to him so before he embarked for good on his glamorous new profession abroad, he turned the responsibility of his teaching over to his head instructor and friend, Danny Inosanto.

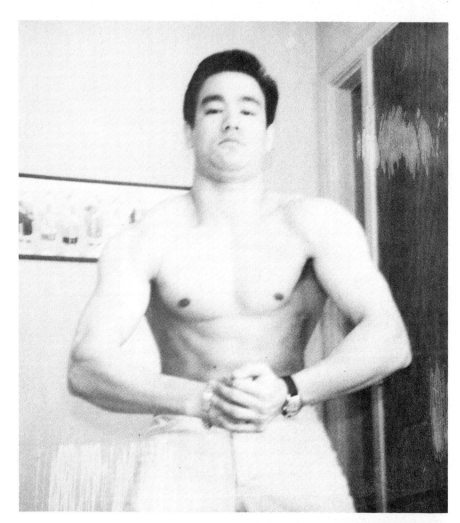

Bruce at age 19, after having started weight training. Not being especially a big person conditioning and power were very important to him.

Impromptu demonstrations of brick-breaking. Phoebe, Bruce's sister recalls, "Bruce loved to break bricks. He often tried to teach me how but I could never seem to learn."

(Top)Bruce at age 20 in Oakland, Calif. beginning to look like the Bruce Lee that millions of martial arts fans all over the world soon come to know and idolize. (Bottom)Bruce giving Robert a few pointers. Robert did not share his brother's great love for the martial arts. He preferred singing and acting and today is not only a popular singer in Hong Kong, but will soon be doing professional film acting.

Bruce believed in regular training sessions. He felt that the more practice one had, the better prepared he would be in case a real situation came up. Bruce regularly would work out with such training aids as the Wing Chun wooden dummy, the air-kicking bag, the focusing mitt and the speed bag. And if Bruce couldn't find the training aid he was looking for, he invented new equipment to use in practice. Although high kicks (top of page) were not used in jeet kune do practice sessions, Bruce always practiced them on the heavy bag because he knew he would have to use them for added excitement in the movies.

(Opposite page) The photos for Bruce's book "Chinese Gung Fu; The Philosophical Art of Self Defense" were shot in the parking lot of Ruby Chow's in Seattle.

32

"The Big Break"

It's a little known fact that Ed Parker, himself a pioneer in American karate, was responsible for Bruce getting the role of Kato in the popular "Green Hornet" television series. When Bruce debuted to the world at Ed Parker's 1964 Internationals, Ed was getting it all down on film. Fate intervened a few years later while Ed was teaching Jay Sebring (one of the people later killed along with Sharon Tate in the Sharon Tate murders). Jay mentioned that his friend Bill Dozier (the producer of "Batman") had bought the rights to the "Green Hornet" and needed a Kato. Parker showed Dozier the film on Bruce and the rest is history.

(Top)As Kato on the popular T.V. series "The Green Hornet", Bruce introduced millions to the beauty, creativity and power of the martial arts. (Left) Bruce in costume signing autographs for his loyal fans.

Kato without his mask.

Bruce clowning around with actor Van Williams, who portrayed The Green Hornet on the show, Williams admired and respected Bruce and became his student and friend.

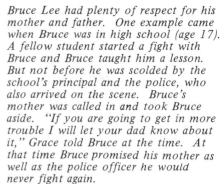

Bruce Lee had plenty of respect for his mother and father. One example came when Bruce was in high school (age 17). A fellow student started a fight with Bruce and Bruce taught him a lesson. But not before he was scolded by the school's principal and the police, who also arrived on the scene. Bruce's mother was called in and took Bruce aside. "If you are going to get in more trouble I will let your dad know about it," Grace told Bruce at the time. At that time Bruce promised his mother as well as the police officer he would never fight again.

Bruce's affection and respect for his parents never waned. In 1965, when Bruce's father died, Bruce flew to Hong Kong from Oakland, Calif. to attend the funeral. Bruce was the first child to arrive at the funeral, and by so doing, custom dictated that he represent the family in the traditional position. So he crawled into the ceremony on his knees, weeping uncontrollably. It was a sign of respect for his father while at the same time asking for forgiveness on behalf of his brothers and sisters.

Jeet Kune Do

In an excerpt from a letter to Dan Inosanto, Bruce expressed his feelings about his art:

"I hope that my thinking on the art will help you in your training, or in choosing what is beneficial and what is futile. Then use your common sense to see what is the real thing and what is the real thing and what is merely lessons in routine dancing.

To me, Gung-Fu is so extraordinary because it is nothing at all special; Gung-Fu is simply the direct expression of one's feelings with the minimum lines and energy—every movement being so of itself, without the artificialities of which 99% of all masters tend to complicate. Always remember that the closer to the true way of Gung-Fu, the less wastage of expression there is. The art is the expression of the self. The more complicated and restrictive the method is, the less the opportunity for the expression of one's original sense of freedom."

Bruce would select his students intuitively. He could size them up almost immediately. And if there was something about them he didn't like, he refused to accept them. Dan Inosanto said that "In organizing his art, he had all the right qualifications. Number one, he had to have been a boxer. He had to have had Wing Chun training to know the center line. He had to have had a brother who was a fencer. He had to have been a street fighter to know what

was functional. He had to have had friends who were in Northern style Gung-fu to develop the legs. He had to have come to America in order to meet boxers and wrestlers to reach yet another stage. He had to have had a personality like Bruce Lee to get ahead."

The Bruce Lee in movies fought very differently than the Bruce Lee fighting for real. When he really fought, there was no expression on his face, just determination. He would look at you coldly through piercing eyes. He called it "controlled cruelty." Some of his

Bruce with close friend and student James Lee outside the Chinatown school. James designed and fashioned many of the innovative training devices that Bruce would later use when he worked out using full power.

Bruce Lee's

JEET KUNE DO

截 拳 道

Professional
Consultation & Instruction............*$275 per Hour*
Ten Sessions Course *$1000*
Instruction Overseas $1000 a week plus expenses

JUN FAN GUNG FU INSTITUTE
振 藩 國 術 館

Using No Way As Way
Having No Limitation As Limitation

favorite expressions regarding his art are as follows:

Bruce referred to rigidly structured martial arts systems as "exercises in futility," "organized despair," and "the Classical mess."

"Practice seriously (not goofing off, seriously studying and learning) but don't seriously practice (no long faces, feel the joy in it)."

"I have no design. I make your intention my design."

Bruce would often say, "I'm only the guide. The fingers pointing to the moon. Don't keep looking at the fingers. The moon is beautiful. You should be striving to see that."

"There is no such thing as maturity. There is maturing. You should always be improving, always moving toward a never-ending perfection."

Bruce did not consider Jeet Kune Do (Way of the Stopping Fist) a style. He thought of it as a method of self-discovery. He didn't want anyone to make a big deal about the name because that's all it was. Later on he was even sorry he named it at all. Jeet Kune Do was like a boat to get you across a river. Once you reached land, he didn't want you to carry the boat on your back. The idea was to continually progress.

He believed in teaching the concept, not the technique. From the concept you can get a lot of techniques. For example, Bruce would ask, "How do you relax? What is relaxation to you?" One guy might say he goes to the beach, another might like to go to the mountains, still another might just like to stay at home and read a book. He would get all different answers but each was valid. In other words, he would teach the concept, and then let the students apply it in the ways that were most workable for them.

He despised "robot training." "Life is everchanging. Don't get caught up in a certain rhythm. Real combat isn't in a set rhythm. You have to be spontaneous and adapt to a kind of broken rhythm, reacting to whatever comes up as it comes up."

When students' movements in class became robotlike because of the repetition, he would stop them

(Top)
Bruce's personal business card listing his fees, though his rates were extremely high, he was always booked solidly.

A sample of one of Bruce's business card that he printed up to help promote his school.

BRUCE LEE'S
TAO OF
CHINESE Gung Fu

USING NO WAY AS WAY≈HAVING NO LIMITATION AS LIMITATION

This sign was one of Bruce's favorite and was hung on the wall of his Chinatown kwoon expressing his philosophy of his art.

This is the membership card used in the early days when his school was called the Jun Fan Gung-Fu Institute. There was a branch in Seattle headed by Taky Kimura, one in Oakland led by James Lee and a third branch in Los Angeles under Dan Inosanto. The cards, certificates and other school literature were artistically designed by Bruce utilizing the Yin Yang symbol with his own modifications.

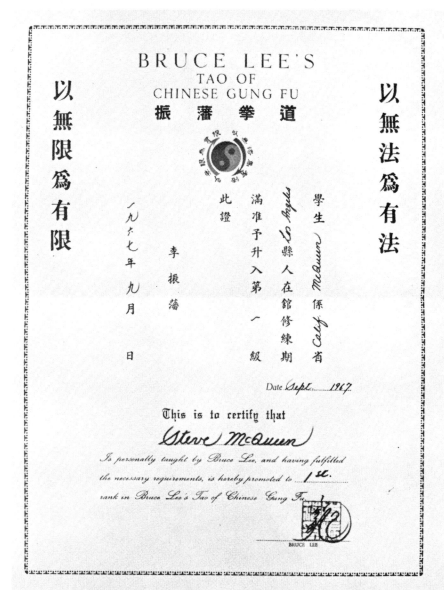

Bruce had a lot of friends and students, but no one received his school's diploma unless they had earned it. Shown here is actor Steve McQueen's diploma of achievement.

immediately. "Look, I don't want to see a hundred lousy punches. All of them put together aren't going to help you if you come up against a guy who can throw one good one."

Bruce believed that there were 3 stages of learning:
1) **Learn**—to consciously learn a technique.
2) **Apply**—to practice the technique until you can successfully apply it.
3) **Dissolve**—When the technique becomes automatic, a part of you.

He also believed that there were only five ways to initiate an attack:
1) **ABC**—attack by combination
2) **ABD**—attack by drawing
3) **HIA**—hand immobilization attack or
   FIA foot immobilization attack
4) **SDA**—single direct attack
5) **SAA**—single angular attack

As a more effective substitute for blocking, Lee perfected what is now referred to as the "trapping hands" stage. Trapping becomes more effective than blocking because there is less wastage of movement, and the opponent's hand is fully immobilized instead of deflected. Its lineage is traceable to his original style, Wing Chun, whose practitioners believe that attack is the best form of defense. They reject the conventional one-two sequence of block then counter-attack in favor of simultaneous blocking and punching, Pak Sau.

Chi Sau or "sticky hands" practice is a form of sparring not unique to Wing Chun, where two opponents face off with forearms barely touching and try to uproot the other while maintaining their own sense of balance. This exercise is repeated over and over in order to perfect hand techniques already learned, toughen the forearm and hands and develop sensitivity. Incorporating Chi Sau and Pak Sau with Bong Sau (deflecting) and Lap Sau (warding off, almost grabbing), Lee came up with "trapping hands."

There were very few photographs taken of Bruce Lee's early Jeet Kune Do classes. This is one from Dan Lee's scrapbook. "During one of our regular workouts, Bruce and Kareem Abdul-Jabber unexpectedly walked in," recalls Dan Lee. "Most of us had never seen Kareem before since he only worked privately with Bruce. His size was so unbelievable that everyone wanted me to take his picture." From left to right, standing are: Chuck Hill, Gary Fineman, Lee Hong, Melvin Kwan, Leo Duffin, Danny Inosanto, Kareem Abdul-Jabbar, Bruce, Larry Hartsell, Bill Bremer, Mike Cochrane, Robert Lujan. Seated: Dan Lee, Pete Rosas, Al Wolin.

Bruce was fanatical about conditioning because of an incident which once occurred in Oakland, California. He accepted a challenge and the outcome at best could be said to have been a "draw." Although his poor showing could largely be attributed to his stubborn insistence upon adhering to his Wing Chun style, he later confessed to Dan Inosanto "I was tired, Dan. I was so tired I couldn't even punch him."

One night, two martial artists showed up at the College St. kwoon in Chinatown. They wanted to fight. Bruce explained that they were in the middle of class and would have to wait till class was over. He motioned for his best student, Dan Lee, to change his position in the line-up so that he was working out directly in front of the two observers. Awestruck, they watched as Dan went all out as he executed his techniques. At break time, Bruce walked up to the two spectators, who appeared visibly shaken by what they had witnessed. Bruce said that if they wanted to fight now, he'd be more than happy to let them spar with his students. They stutteringly declined the invitation, bowed politely, and left. This type of psychology was typical of Bruce's philosophy of combat and he referred to it as "winning the war

without firing a shot."

However, Danny Inosanto said that at times Bruce could be the most mature person he'd ever met and at other times he could be the most childish.

Bruce's biggest flaw was his temper. His temper literally frightened me and not too many people frighten me. One night, after a class, Dan Lee, Bruce, and I were in Bruce's kitchen. Bruce brought out some boxing gloves and playfully challenged Dan to put them on. They started jabbing at each other in fun, and then all of a sudden Dan got in a lucky punch. Bruce, who believed himself to be "untouchable," went berserk and completely lost control, ferociously attacking Dan. This continued until Bruce gradually cooled down. Dan just tried to block and dodge his punches as best he could and I didn't say a word. Later, as I was packing up my stuff and getting ready to leave, Bruce said, "You didn't like what I did, did you, Danny?" I pretended I didn't hear him. He asked again louder, "You didn't like it, did you??" Again I didn't answer. Finally, he said, "Doggone, Danny, you hear me. Quit making like you don't hear me!!" He then explained to me that he just couldn't hold back. He knew he

shouldn't be doing it but he just couldn't stop himself. He told me that if there was one thing he could change about himself, it would have been his bad temper.

He also remembers Bruce as always being very generous. "One time we were in a sporting goods store and I saw a set of weights I wanted to buy but I only had twelve dollars on me. I said I'd have to wait till next week to buy them. Bruce said that while he was there he should probably buy a set of weights for Brandon (his son). He did buy a set and when I was about to leave his home that day he told me to take the weights with me. He had really bought them for *me*, not Brandon."

Dan Inosanto said "He continually amazed me. I mean, he could literally do four things at one time. He would read a book, watch TV, have his leg

Bruce standing outside the Chinatown school with his faithful companion, Bobo.

This photo of Bruce's hand is one example of his liberation from the "classical mess." The enlarged knuckles clearly define the striking area of his fist, contrary to most tradional martial art rules, where impact is focused on the first two knuckles.

Bruce with close friend and associate Dan Inosanto. Dan appeared in Bruce's last movie Game Of Death. *Here they take time out to go over a fighting scene using Dan's favorite weapon— the escrima stick.*

fully extended in a high side kick and hold the position, while carrying on a conversation with me. How could anyone have even the slightest chance against him in a fight if he was concentrating solely on his opponent?"

He wound up working with machines and wooden dummies because no one could give him a really good workout. And it was far too dangerous for him to go all out with anyone.

By the way, Danny Inosanto, who trained regularly with probably the deadliest martial artist the world has ever known, is a schoolteacher by day and teaches English and Social Studies. What's ironic here is that he used to teach Driver's Education but quit because he felt it was too dangerous.

Hong Kong and Superstardom

In 1971, Bruce went to Thailand to star in "The Big Boss". Hong Kong fans absolutely loved it. His second movie "Fists of Fury" was even more successful.

Dan Lee, one of Bruce's best students, said "When 'Big Boss' was released in Hong Kong, Bruce would slip into movie theatres unnoticed and sit in the first row to watch the audience reaction. In Hong Kong, audiences are very critical because they've seen so many kung-fu movies and don't react unless they see something they feel to be really special. He was a little apprehensive, but after a few scenes the audience would generally go crazy, applauding wildly and jumping out of their seats."

Bruce then formed his own production company in association with Raymond Chow and together they produced "Way of the Dragon". "Enter the Dragon" came next and Bruce predicted it would be more successful than all the others. His judgement proved as accurate as his kicks and punches and the film was a fantastic success.

It didn't seem as if anything could stop Bruce Lee now and everyone felt he was going to go all the way. Unfortunately, this was not to be the case. On July 20, 1973, when Bruce's newest project "Game of Death" was only partially completed, he died suddenly at the age of thirty-two.

Bruce breaking boards with one of his devastating sidekicks.

Bruce loved to talk about his art. He was always a welcome guest on Hong Kong television shows.

(Opposite page)Bruce with son Brandon watching a martial arts demonstration in Hong Kong.

49

Bruce was always energetic, perhaps, too energetic. He couldn't sit still. In fact, when he was around people, he didn't care if he had on his jacket or not. He would start jabbing, punching and bouncing. He figured there was never anything more important than practice.

(below) Bruce was known for the speed in which he demonstrated in his techniques. Several times he would challenge someone to a test of speed. Bruce would take one step forward and touch his opponent's face before his opponent could even touch Bruce's hand.

His return to Hong Kong brought Bruce the recognition he had long been seeking. Almost overnight he became a celebrity. It was not unusual to turn on the tele-vision and see Bruce on a talk show demonstrating his ability to do one fingered push ups along with some techniques of Jeet Kune Do.

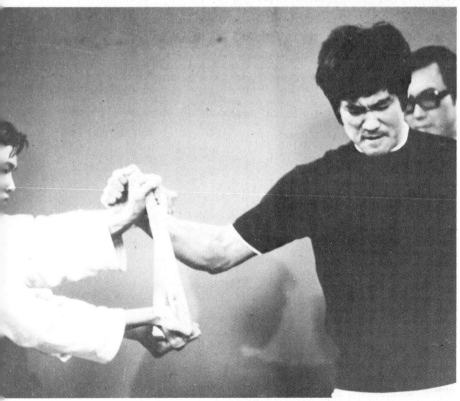

Always being asked questions, Bruce never hesitated to share his education with those interested in finding out about him and the martial arts. Left: Bruce demonstrates his famous one-inch punch. "The power is generated from the entire body to the focus point like a shock from a earthquake," he once said.

Bruce flanked by two popular Hong Kong actresses.

Bruce is shown here with movie producer Raymond Chow(left) and friend. Bruce later joined up with Chow to form a production company called Concorde Productions in Hong Kong.

Bruce playfully executes one of his devastating side kicks in an impromptu sparring session with a friend in a Hong Kong restaurant.

Bruce being interviewed in Hong Kong.

(Below) As a child, Bruce could never sit still even for a minute. He never changed, in this photo, sitting and trying to relax, he looks extremely restless as if he was about to burst into motion at any moment.

Bruce with his mother, son Brandon, and
a close friend in Hong Kong.
It wasn't until 1965 that Grace first saw
Bruce's wife Linda and son Brandon.
Bruce and Linda were married in 1964
in the United States but Bruce's parents
were still in Hong Kong. A year later
when Brandon was three months old,
came the first visit to Grace.

Bruce with older brother Peter in 1970.
They were always very close.

Bruce in a Hong Kong park with sister-in-law Sylvia in 1970. Bruce playfully spars with Sylvia and gives her some pointers on self defense.

"Fists of Fury" includes a scene where a large menacing dog attacks Bruce. Lo Wei, the film's director, knew exactly what he wanted the scene to look like on camera, but capturing the effect was very difficult because split second timing was essential. Here we see crew members hurling the animal at Bruce and Bruce leaping up and out of the way just in the nick of time.

Bruce with "Fists of Fury" director Lo Wei, in Hong Kong.

On location at the Roman Coliseum during the production of Way Of The Dragon, *Bruce goes over the finer points of martial arts filming with Chuck Norris, Bob Wall, actress Ting Pei and Hong Kong's "Little Unicorn."*

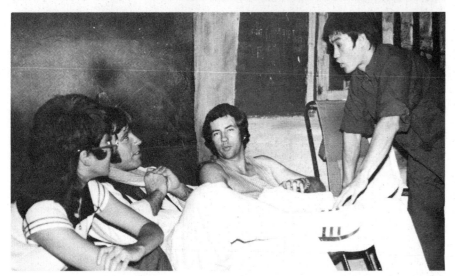

THE LEGEND ON SCREEN

After the "Green Hornet" and "Longstreet" television series, Bruce was asked to star in the television series "Kung-Fu." Bruce thought about it but decided he wasn't a good enough actor for the American market at the time. Instead, he went to Hong Kong to make a series of action movies, which propelled him into international superstardom. As time went on, Bruce was determined to upgrade his films. Eventually he incorporated his philosophy and jeet kune do into his films.

Fist of Fury *originally titled* The Chinese Connection *was a typical low budget "chop-suey" film. Bruce was reluctant to have this film shown in the Western market because of it's lack of sophistication. His charisma and martial arts ability overshadowed any short comings in the film and instantly catapulted him to superstar status.*

FISTS OF FURY

With the box office success of Fist Of Fury *behind him, Bruce asserted more of himself in each succeeding film. In* The Chinese Connection *his fight scenes were flawless and believable. His simple and direct fighting style of Jeet Kune Do would set the standard for all martial arts films to come.*

THE CHINESE CONNECTION

Way Of The Dragon, *his third film, was a total Bruce Lee production. He wrote it, directed it, cast it and chose the locations. It was unheard of for a Chinese production company to go to the expense of filming in the famed Coliseum in Rome. Chuck Norris, the famous American martial artist, was flown in to make the fight scenes still more exciting and to give this film a true international flavor.*

WAY OF THE DRAGON

ENTER THE DRAGON

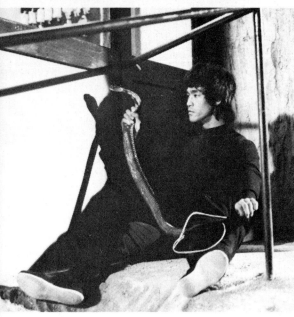

Enter The Dragon *is considered by many to be the ultimate martial arts film of all time. Major motion picture stars along with American cinematography techniques were featured. Bruce also showed his weapons ability with the nunchaku and the Filipino double sticks This was also the only film using his own voice.*

While filming in Hong Kong, he began to lose weight because of the humidity, the amount of energy it took to execute the techniques properly and because he wanted to get involved in many aspects of filmmaking. But even though he weighed only 128 pounds towards the end of his career, he still had the power, speed and respect to make him one of the top martial artist around. For a person his size, he could still punch faster and harder than most heavyweights.

Bruce Lee, thanks to the help of instructor Dan Inosanto, became proficient at using the nunchaku and escrima sticks. "Bruce was a natural in the martial arts," says Inosanto. "He would perfect the use of weapons in a week's time after he was shown how to use them. He would always work on various camera angles for the fight scenes involving weapons. He would work for hours at a time on them to perfect the scenes. He always wanted the audience to get their money's worth."

GAME OF DEATH

"The Game of Death" was to be his crowning achievement, and would have been if he were around to complete it. He wanted to show his gratitude to his former students and instructors by including them in this film. Dan Inosanto was his Filipino-style opponent, Taky Kimura, unable to attend, was to have been his Preying Mantis opponent and Kareem Abdul-Jabbar was his unknown style opponent.

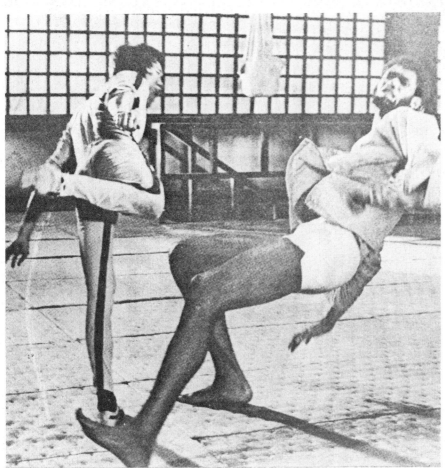

After the "Game Of Death" movie, which involved Bruce in a fight sequence with Los Angeles Laker Kareem Abdul Jabbar, Bruce was scheduled to sign a contract with producer Run Run Shaw for another action film. Bruce had promised Shaw his next film because it was Shaw who gave Bruce his first big break in the movies. Unfortunately that movie never came to pass.

On Bruce Lee's Death

Upon hearing the news of her son's death, Grace Lee literally didn't believe it. Several months before, stories had begun appearing in Hong Kong magazines that "Bruce Lee Is Dead." Grace would immediately call Hong Kong to see if the stories were true. They never were. When she told Bruce how much the stories upset her, Bruce would always say they were only written to sell magazines. "He told me that the next time I hear a story like that not to believe it because it won't be true. Then one day one of my friends called me up. She was crying and told me she had heard Bruce was dead. I told her it was a mistake. Bruce told me that the magazines always say that. Then my friend told me she hadn't read it in a magazine. She had heard it on television. A little later we found out it was true."

Bruce's sister Agnes was also in a state of shocked disbelief. "He had always been so healthy. But he had been working very hard and had collapsed a few months earlier while working on a film. After I learned he had died, I couldn't eat or sleep for months."

Phoebe, Bruce's other sister, was also stunned. "He had told me that he'd been working very hard but I guess none of us realized how hard. He said that after he finished "Game of Death," he was going to take a long rest."

Adding to the shock of Bruce's family, friends, and millions of fans was the inquest verdict itself. "Death by misadventure" was at best a ludicrously cryptic explanation. Doctors finally agreed that death was due to a cerebral edema (water on the brain), but none could pinpoint the precise factor that caused it.

Some intimates felt that by stubbornly adhering to his long and intensely rigorous daily training schedule even in Hong Kong's steamy climate, he eventually just burned himself out.

Another thought is that he'd had an allergic reaction to the medication he was taking for his injured back. A more bizarre variation on this theory was that he had unknowingly been administered an untraceable oriental poison.

Continuing along those lines, another story sprang up that a rival master had given him what was known in martial arts legends as the "death touch." Danny Inosanto, Bruce's close friend and associate, thought this theory was especially absurd because he firmly believed that nobody could get close enough to Bruce to even attempt something like that.

Still more exotic were the rumors that Bruce was murdered by the Chinese Mafia or greedy film producers he refused to work with.

To this day, many questions remain unanswered, and an aura of mystery still and probably always will surround the death of Bruce Lee.

Bruce Lee Day

On June 7, 1979, "Game of Death", Bruce Lee's last movie, premiered at the Paramount Theatre on Hollywood Boulevard, and well over a thousand loyal fans attended, joyously paying homage to their idol. Garbed in traditional martial arts uniforms, they stood outside on the street, holding their school banners high and with great pride.

One of the highlights of the evening was when Bruce's son Brandon unveiled a thirty foot long display containing original costumes and weapons from his father's most exciting film roles.

When the master of ceremonies read Mayor Tom Bradley's proclamation of Bruce Lee Day, the crowd burst into applause and cheered wildly.

Also on hand were Bruce's mother, his widow, close friend Dan Inosanto (who appeared in the film), Colleen Camp (the film's feminine lead), Mel Novak (one of the film's bad guys), and Joe Lewis, a prominent martial arts figure.

Bruce Lee literally became a legend in his own time. True, he no longer walks among us, but legends never really die. He will live on forever!

*Simplicity is the last step of art, and the
beginning of nature. Be soft yet not
yielding; firm, yet not hard.*
BRUCE LEE